Games with
Rope and String

THE MARSHALL CAVENDISH ILLUSTRATED GUIDE TO
GAMES CHILDREN PLAY AROUND THE WORLD

Games with Rope and String

Ruth Oakley

Illustrated by Steve Lucas

Marshall Cavendish
New York · London · Toronto · Sydney

Library Edition 1989

Published by Marshall Cavendish Corporation
147 West Merrick Road
Freeport
Long Island
N.Y. 11520

Produced by DPM Services Limited
Designed by Graham Beehag

Library of Congress Cataloging-in-Publication Data

Oakley, Ruth.
   Games with rope and string/written by Ruth Oakley: Illustrated
by Steve Lucas.
      p.   cm. — (Games children play).
   Includes index.
   Summary: Describes a number of games involving rope and string.
   ISBN 1-85435-081-1:
   1. String figures — Juvenile literature. [1. String figures. 2. Games.] I.
Lucas, Steve [1]. II. Title. III. Series: Oakley, Ruth. Games children play.
GV1218.S8025 1989
793'.9 — dc19   88-28709
                                                                      CIP
                                                                       AC

ISBN 1-85435-076-5

Printed and bound in Italy by L.E.G.O. SpA, Vicenza

Contents

Jumping rope is an activity which some adults do as part of a fitness and training program for another sport or just as a healthy activity which is fun in its own right. It has also been enjoyed by generations of children in most countries who have used their ingenuity to find something to skip with.

Rope was one of man's first inventions, and cord made from flax which dates back to 1000 B.C. has been found. Cave paintings of an even earlier date have also been discovered which show men climbing something like a rope ladder. Many museums have examples of rope; the British Museum has pieces of rope made from Nile reeds which are

Boxers often skip as part of their training to get fit.

Indians used wild grapevines to make jump ropes.

about 2,000 years old. Rope and string used to be made from various plants such as jute, sisal, cotton, and coir, but nowadays, many are made of synthetic fibers such as nylon.

Perhaps some of the earliest and simplest jump ropes were strong creeping vines from the plants in the forest. Cherokee Indians use wild grapevines, and people in Barbados also use vines. Plaited straw was used in Hungary, and leather was cut

7

into strips in New Zealand. Hop vines were used in Kent in England.

Also in England, sash windows were used in most buildings from the eighteenth century until well into the twentieth, and generations of English children used sash cord as jump ropes. In parts of the north of England where there were cotton mills, the worn-out bobbins from the weaving machines were sometimes used as handles for jump ropes.

This English cottage has sash windows.

Jump rope made from sash cord and bobbins.

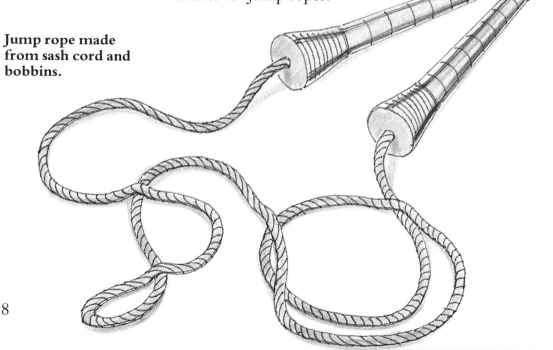

A great variety of jump ropes can be bought now. There are very sophisticated ones with built-in counters, or you can use a piece of heavy cord and knot the ends. A length of plastic-coated clothesline will do as well. To check that the rope is the correct length for you, hold one end in each hand and stand on the rope. It should be taut when you hold your hands, and the ends, up under your armpits.

The basic skipping step is just to jump up and down on the spot while passing the rope under your feet and over your head. When you have mastered this, you can go on to fancy steps, such as pointing your toe, tapping your heel, and bending your knees. You can also vary the way you swing the rope, such as swinging it to one side or folding your arms so that the rope crosses itself.

The correct length of rope.

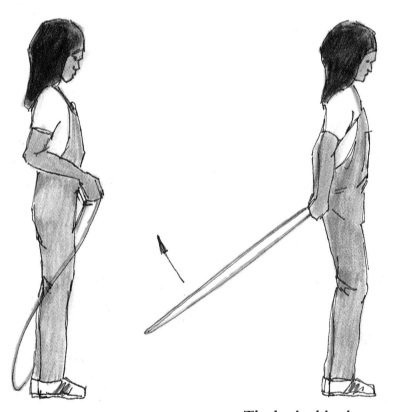

The basic skipping step.

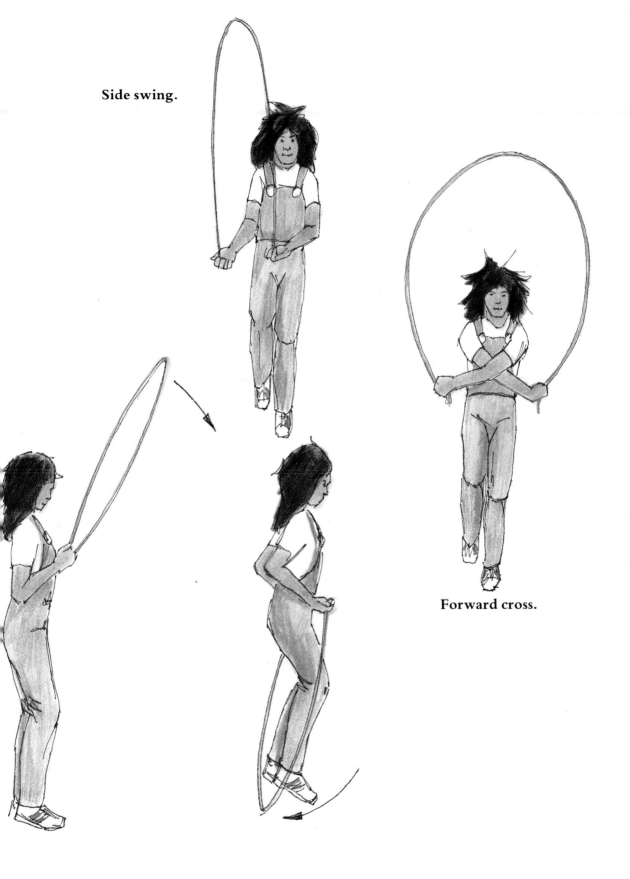

Side swing.

Forward cross.

Bumps is a very fast step. The skipper jumps up high so that the rope passes twice under the skipper's feet during one turn of the rope. A good rhyme for this is:

R. White's ginger beer goes off pop.
Penny on the bottle when you take it to the
S-H-O-P, shop.

You do the bumps as you spell out the letters.

In the past, there was a deposit of a penny to pay on a large bottle of soda pop, and children used to like to take the empty bottles back to the shop so that they could claim the penny and spend it on candy.

Another fast rhyme is:

Salt, mustard, vinegar, pepper.
Salt, mustard, vinegar, PEPPER.

Visiting is when you jump and someone else runs in and jumps in your rope with you.

Jumping by yourself can be fun, but there are lots of rhymes and actions you can do in a group with your friends if you have a long piece of rope. It needs to be about four yards long and fairly heavy. Two people turn the rope for the rest and everybody chants the words. An easy one to start with is

Keep the Kettle Boiling, which is also known as Chase the Fox, or Running Through. The first person runs through the rope while it is turning and everyone else follows. Then the first person jumps once and runs out, and everyone else copies this. Then the first player jumps twice and runs out, and everyone else does the same. Then she takes three jumps, and so on. If a player steps on the rope or makes a mistake, he is out, and the game continues until only one jumper is left.

All in Together, Girls is another simple one to start with.
The rope is turned and everybody stands outside it chanting.

 All in together, girls.
 This fine weather, girls.
 January, February, March, April, May. . . .
and so on through the months of the year.

 Each person jumps into the rope when her birthday month
is called out and stays in until everyone is jumping in the rope.
Then, the verse is changed to:

 All OUT together, girls.
 This fine weather, girls. . . .
and each child runs out on the appropriate month.

A jump rope game with actions is **Teddy Bear, Teddy Bear.** The game usually begins with one person running into the rope and doing all the actions right through. Then, the next player runs in and

they both go through the routine, and so on until everyone is in the rope. Usually, someone goes wrong, and the challenge is to get everyone to do it correctly all the way to the end!

Teddy bear, teddy bear, touch the ground.
Teddy bear, teddy bear, turn around.
Teddy bear, teddy bear, touch your shoes.
Teddy bear, teddy bear, pay your dues.
Teddy bear, teddy bear, go upstairs.
Teddy bear, teddy bear, say your prayers.
Teddy bear, teddy bear, switch off the light.
Teddy bear, teddy bear, say GOODNIGHT.

At the last GOODNIGHT, everyone runs out of the rope together.

English girls play **I am a Girl Guide** in the same way.

I am a Girl Guide dressed in blue.
These are the actions I must do.
Salute to the King, and bow to the Queen.
Stand at ease and bend my knees.
Twist right round and count fifteen.
One, two, three, four. . . .

A French rhyme is:

Ou vas-tu, petit soldat?
Je pars pour la guerre.
Que portes-tu dans t'sac?
Des pommes de terre.

Which means

Where are you going, little soldier?
I am going to war.
What are you carrying in your sack?
Potatoes!

Some of the rhymes can be used to tell fortunes in the same way that some people count the cherry stones on their plates. The questions are "answered" when the jumper trips in the rope.

A rosy apple, a lemon or a tart,
Tell me the name of your sweetheart.
A, B, C, D, E, F. . . . (continue until the jumper misses).
Will he marry me?
Yes, no, yes, no. . . .
What will you go to the wedding in?
A wheelbarrow, a horse and cart,
A sidecar, a motor car. . . .
What will your wedding dress be made of?
Silk, satin, cotton, rags. . . .

There are several more traditional verses, but you could bring it up to date by making up your own questions and possible answers to choose from.

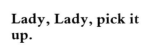

Lady, Lady, pick it up.

16

In this rhyme, the "letter" that is dropped is a stone and then the next person jumps in the rope and picks it up.

Early in the morning at half past eight,
I hear the postman at the gate.
Postman, postman, drop your letter.
Lady, lady, pick it up.

The idea of this game is for the next player to run in as the previous one runs out.

As I was in the kitchen doing a bit of stitching,
In walked the bogeyman and I walked out.

If you really want a challenge, you can try doing this **Double Dutch**, which means having two ropes turning at once in opposite directions. Another variation is **French Dutch**, which is jumping with your own short rope inside a long rope turned by two other people. You might like to work out a routine of fancy steps with your friends and give a demonstration.

A game with a rope which is played in Ghana is **A-Fishing**.
It is a group game that can be played in a large space indoors or
outside. Two parallel lines are drawn about four yards apart
for the shore, and four fishermen are chosen and given a long
piece of rope. The rest of the players run through the "water"
making swimming movements as if they were fish in the sea.
Sometimes, the fishermen sing a song, and at the end of the
song, they encircle as many of the fish as they can with the
rope. You could just have a signal if you wanted, or you could
make up your own song. The winner is the last fish to be
caught.

Another popular game with a rope is played in many
places. One person crouches in the middle of a circle of chil-

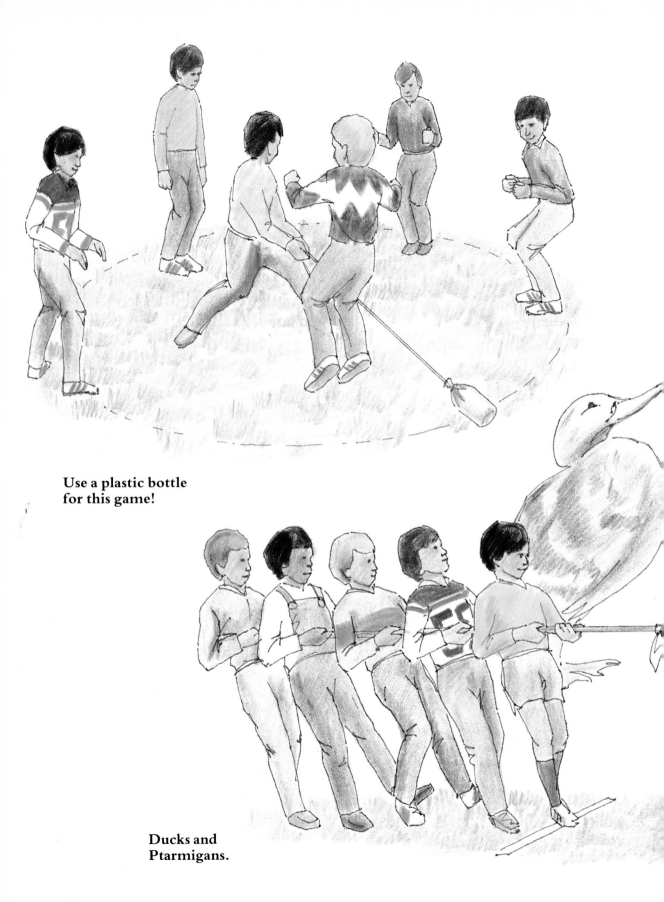

Use a plastic bottle
for this game!

Ducks and
Ptarmigans.

20

dren who are standing. The crouching player turns around and around holding a piece of rope for the others to jump over. If anyone touches the rope, she is out. The last player standing is the winner.

Another rope activity that is popular around the world is a Tug of War. These contests often take place at village fetes in England, where they are usually performed by young men who take them very seriously. Children can play the game in an informal and lighthearted way. You need a piece of strong rope about four yards long and ten or more children in two equal teams. Mark the middle of the rope with some yarn or a piece of material tied around it, and agree two marks on the ground over which the marker has to pass before either side has won.

Then every member of both teams takes hold of the rope, one behind the other. The heaviest team member is usually

put at the back of the line, at the end of the rope. On a given signal, everyone pulls as hard as possible until one side or the other manages to pull the marker to the agreed position. If you have not got a rope, you can play this game just by holding each other around the waist and pulling.

As with so many traditional games, Tug of War probably originated as a ceremonial or religious activity. In Japan, villages used to compete in a rope-pulling contest to guarantee a good harvest, using a rope made of woven straw.

The Eskimos also have a kind of Tug or War at the beginning of winter. The two sides are known as "Ptarmigans" and "Ducks." The Ptarmigans are the people and children whose birthdays fall in the winter, and the Ducks are the people of summer. The rope is made of sealskin. The contest is supposed to decide how hard the winter will be. The Ptarmigans

represent the cold, as they are the resident birds who brave the cold weather, and the Ducks are the birds which only fly north for the summer. If the Ptarmigans win, the winter will be a harsh one.

Other American Indians play this game as well, but they call their teams "Winter" and "Summer."

A game called **Crick–Crack Crocodile** from Gambia is a kind of Tug of War, but with three teams. One team is the Crocodile, and they hold onto a pole which has ropes tied on each end. The game begins with the pole across a line marked in the middle of the playing area. The other two teams catch hold of the ropes and try to pull the "crocodile" into their territory, which is marked by goal posts. The end of the string has to be looped over the goal post before either side can claim victory.

Saxon and Dragon is another English version of Tug of War which dates back to the Viking invasion of Saxon England when they came in their curved longships.

A strong wooden stake is driven firmly into the ground, and the middle of a rope is fastened to it using a special knot called a clove hitch. The two sides are called "Saxons" and "Dragons," and the object of the game is to pull the stake out of the ground and drag the opposing team over the middle line.

Viking warrior and longship.

24

One of the oldest ways of playing with a rope, and one which never seems to lose its popularity, is to make a swing. The simplest way is to throw a rope over a strong branch of a tree and knot it securely to make a "seat" to sit on. Get an adult to help you, because you could hurt yourself or damage the tree if you choose a weak branch or do not knot the rope safely.

**Check the knots
very carefully.**

Alternatively, tie an old tire on the end of the rope or make a climbing rope by tying knots at regular intervals, but **ALWAYS ASK AN ADULT TO CHECK IT FOR YOU.**

In parts of Asia, men used to swing as part of religious festivals and at harvest times. In Bolivia, people used to believe that if they could snatch a branch from a tree while swinging on All Souls' Day on November 1, a soul would be released from purgatory. There is an old children's rhyme which goes:

One to Earth and one to Heaven,
And THIS to carry my soul to Heaven.

When the swinger said "THIS," he tried to touch a branch.

A more modern game, and one which is played in countries as far apart as Hong Kong and Ireland, is called **Chinese Straddle Jump**. You need a piece of narrow elastic about three yards long, or you can loop together a number of strong rubber bands.

In the English version, also called **French Skipping**, two children stand with the elastic, which is joined into a loop, around their legs so that it is about six inches above the ground and taut enough to stay in place. The player who is going to do the jumping stands with both feet inside the elastic and jumps in and out of the loop in an agreed sequence. A simple possibility is this:

Jump up and over the elastic and land with one foot on each side of the elastic, but outside it. Jump again and land with both feet inside as you began (Fig. 1).

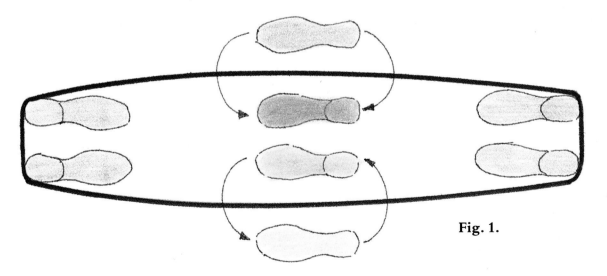

Fig. 1.

Jump out of the elastic, turning your body as you do so that you land with both feet outside the elastic on the same side and facing toward it (Fig. 2).

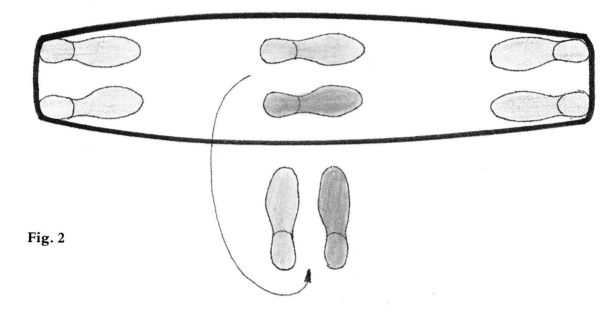

Fig. 2

With the elastic in front of your legs, jump over the farthest side of the loop so that you take the nearest side of the loop over it (Fig. 3).

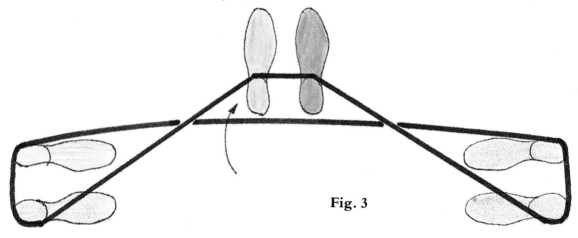

Fig. 3

Jump and make a quarter-turn so that you are parallel to the loop again. Jump again and spread your feet out to make Fig. 4. Now try to jump out, but be warned: this jump is difficult.

Fig. 4

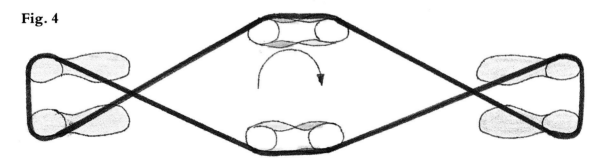

Each person has a turn until they make a mistake or catch the elastic. If a player gets through the elastic at ankle level, then it is raised to shin level and then to the knees.

You can make up your own moves if you wish, and you can make it more complicated and turn your body around a full turn as you jump.

In Hong Kong, the elastic is not made into a loop, but it is held at each end. Pass one foot under the elastic as you jump on the other foot, so that the elastic becomes looped around your ankles. Then jump and unravel yourself again.

Pin the Tail on the Donkey is a party game for all ages. Draw the outline of a donkey with no tail on a large piece of cardboard or poster paper, and hang or prop it up at eye level. Make a tail out of a thick string, and put a thumbtack at one end. Each player in turn is blindfolded, turned around several times, and then led up to the donkey. He has to try to place the donkey's tail in the correct position. Mark the initials of each player at the spot he chooses; the player who is the nearest to the correct spot is the winner.

The Japanese play a similar game called **Fukuwarai** during

their New Year celebrations. They draw the outline of a face, and the blindfolded players have to place its features in the correct places.

Apple-on-a-String is a traditional Halloween custom. Apples, one for each child, are threaded on pieces of string, which are hung from the top of the door frame. Or the strings can be tied to a piece of rope, which can then be tied up between two hooks at the level of the faces of the children who are playing. The players then try to bite the apples, but they must not touch them with their hands. Taking a bite is quite difficult and can take a long time because the apples keep bobbing about on the strings. When a child manages to take a bite, the apple can be taken down and eaten normally.

No hands!

A popular game in Britain in the fall is **Conkers**. The nuts from horse-chestnut trees start to fall at this time (especially with the help of children, who throw broken branches up into the trees to dislodge the spiny, green cases in which the nuts are stored). When they are fresh and new, the "conkers" are fairly soft and have a beautiful, glossy, wood-colored sheen. To be good for playing conkers, they need to be left to harden. Some people even bake them in the oven or soak them in vinegar. When you have selected the conker of your choice, carefully bore a hole through it with a skewer. Thread a piece of string through the hole, and secure it underneath with a knot.

You are then ready to challenge someone to a game. Decide who is to start, and then take turns to try to hit your opponent's conker with yours until one of them breaks.

A rhyme to decide who has first go is:

Obli o, my first go!
Obli onker, my first conker!

The player whose conker is being hit wraps the string around his hand, holds the conker out at arm's length, and keeps it perfectly still. The child trying to hit it steadies and aims his own conker by holding the string over his thumb and then flicking his thumb. Usually, the players take turns until one of the conkers breaks.

If both of the conkers were new ones, the winning conker becomes a "one-er." If the conker that was broken had previously won other contests, the scores are added together. A "two-er" which beats a "six-er" would become an "eight-er."

Sometimes, the strings become tangled. Then, the first player to call out, "Strings," has an extra shot.

The name "Conkers" may have originally been "Conquerors," and other nuts are used in other countries.

Ring on a String is a game which is played in South America and Guyana as well as Britain. The players, which can be any number between ten and thirty, sit in a circle on the ground with both hands loosely holding a long piece of string which has been tied together to make a continuous loop. On the string is a ring, or any small object with a hole in the middle, which has previously been threaded on it. In England, children used to use a curtain ring, but any kind of ring, or a shell with a hole in it, would do just as well.

One player stands in the middle and shuts her eyes, while the others decide which child is to start, with the ring con-

Keep your hands moving.

cealed in one of her hands as she holds the string. When this has been arranged, the player in the middle opens her eyes, and the children in the circle keep up a continuous motion of moving their hands apart and together again, so that they touch each others' hands and pass the ring from one player to the next without being seen.

The child in the middle has to watch very carefully and name the person she thinks has the ring. When she guesses correctly, the one who had the ring becomes the next guesser in the middle of the circle.

A game for two is to make a "telephone" with a piece of string and two empty tin cans. In addition to the cans, you need a small nail, a hammer, and a piece of thin cotton string about five yards long.

Remove the lids from the cans carefully. Use a can opener so that the rim is smooth with no jagged edges to cut you. Wash the can thoroughly and dry it carefully. Using the hammer and nail, make a hole in the center of the bottom of each can. Thread the piece of string through the cans, and knot it inside each can. The string must touch the can. If one player stands in one room and speaks into her can while you stand in the next room with the can against your ear so that the string is held taut, you will be able to have a telephone conversation!

Squash Blossoms made from string or yarn were first made by North American Indians who wove them when the crops were growing to encourage a good harvest.

You need two thin sticks about 10 inches long which you cross and tie securely in the middle with yarn or string. Then wind the yarn around the sticks in a kind of square spiral, fas-

Keep the string taut.

A Squash Blossom.

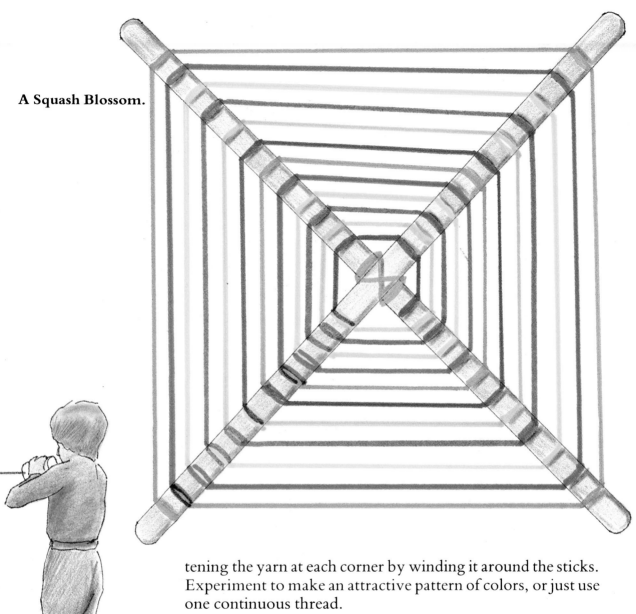

tening the yarn at each corner by winding it around the sticks. Experiment to make an attractive pattern of colors, or just use one continuous thread.

If each member of a group make one, then you can play a game throwing them all at once from one player to the next.

There are few countries in the world where you cannot find some form of string games played on the hands. Some of them were originally believed to have magic powers to help the crops grow, but they have a fascination for most children, and many adults, as a test of skill. Some of them are played alone: others, such as **English Cat's Cradle**, are games for two or more.

In Japan, these games are called **ayatori**. The Germans call them **Hexenspiel**, which means Witch's Game. The Eskimos made many complicated figures, and the Maori people of New Zealand tell stories to match their figures as they make them.

To make string figures, you need a piece of fairly thin string or thick yarn two yards long. If you are not very tall, your arms may not be long enough to manage a loop that long, so shorten the string. Knot the string to make a loop; a square knot is best.

To tie a square knot, hold one end of the string in your left hand and the other in your right hand. Take the right-hand end over and under the left-hand end. (This will mean that the ends have changed hands.) Now, take the left-hand end over and under the right-hand end, and pull them both to make a flat knot which will not slip.

To make a Cat's Cradle, there are at least two basic methods. For the simplest, begin by holding the string as in Figures 1 and 2. Then, with your middle finger, pick up the string from across your palms on the opposite hands (Figures 3 and 4).

If you want to try the alternate method, begin with the loop around the backs of your hands as in Figure 5. Bring the four fingers of one hand over the edge of the loop which is by your thumb and up through the loop. Repeat with the other hand so that your string looks like Figure 6. Then, with your middle finger, pick up the string which is lying across your palm. Repeat with the other hand; you should have a pattern like Figure 7.

To turn the Cradle into the Bed, a partner takes the crosses of the Cradle between her fingers and thumbs and lifts them out and over the straight strings and brings them up through the middle. See Figures 8 and 9.

To turn the Bed into the Candles, the partner takes the crosses of the Bed between fingers and thumbs and lifts them up and over the straight strings and up through the middle again (Figures 10 and 11).

To turn the Candles into the Manger, the partner picks up each of the inside strings with a little finger and crosses them over the outside strings, bringing index fingers and thumbs up through the middle. (Figures 12 and 13).

If you want to find out more about string games, there are several books on the subject, but the easiest way to learn is to ask other people to show you the ones they know.

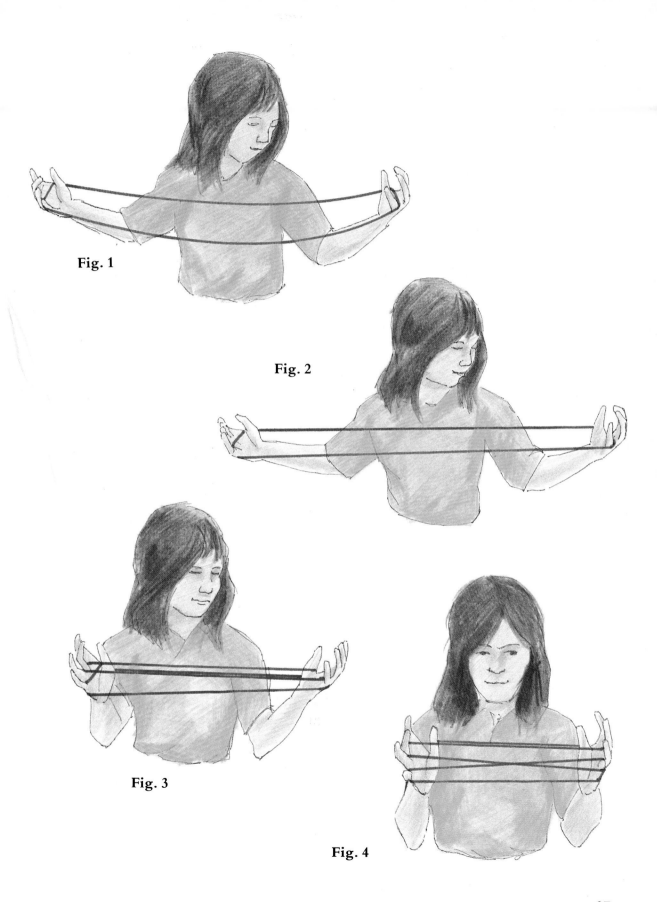

Fig. 1

Fig. 2

Fig. 3

Fig. 4

37

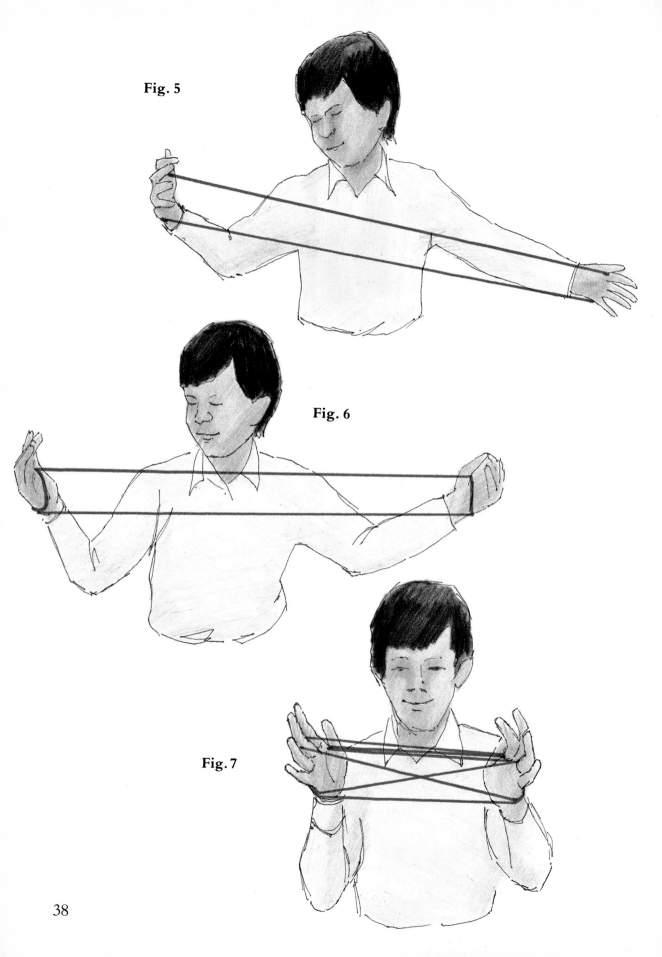

Fig. 5

Fig. 6

Fig. 7

38

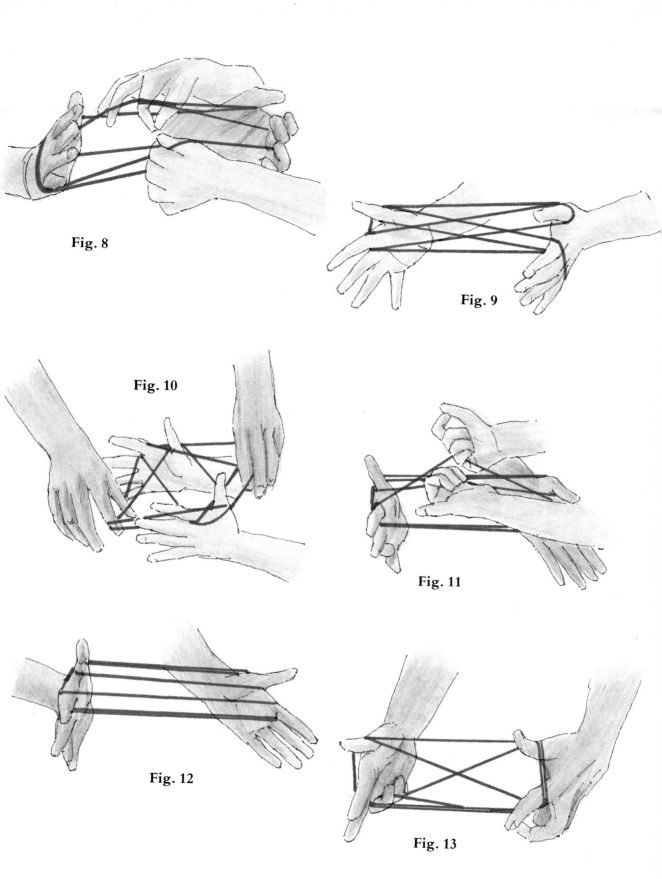

Fig. 8

Fig. 9

Fig. 10

Fig. 11

Fig. 12

Fig. 13

39

A game for one person is **The Parachute**. Other names for this figure are The Bunch of Keys, or A Bunch of Tallow Candles. Tallow candles were long candles made of animal fat which were held in a bunch by their wicks.

1. Place the string on your hand as shown in Figure 1.
2. Hold the string in front of your three middle fingers and pull it toward you (Figure 2).

Fig. 1

Fig. 2

Fig. 3

Fig. 4

3. Take the straight string which is now lying across your palm and pull it toward you. Your string should now look like Figure 3.
4. With your free hand, go inside the large loop which is hanging down, and with one finger pick up the outside edge of the loop around your little finger (Figure 4). Still

41

holding this, pick up the outside edge of the loop around your thumb as well, and gently pull them both through the large loop so that you get Figure 5.

5. Bend over your index, middle, and third fingers into the three rows made by the straight lines and pass the two long loops back over your fingers so that you get Figure 6.

Fig. 5 **Fig. 6**

6. Gently, but firmly, pull the straight string farthest away from your fingers, and you will get the parachute shape in Figure 7.

The Bunch of Candles is made by slipping the loops off the fingers and holding the pattern upside down by the long single loop.

Fig. 7

If you have a piece of string about two yards long and a piece of thick cardboard, you can make a **Whirrer** to amuse a younger child — although you will probably want to do one for yourself as well!

Using a saucer as a guide, draw and cut out a circle from cardboard. With the points of the scissors, carefully pierce two small holes or slits about half an inch apart in the middle of the disc. Thread the string through them, and tie it securely into a loop with a square knot.

Hold up the fingers of one hand and slip one end of the string loop over all four fingers. Take the other end of the loop in the other hand between the thumb and index finger and keep turning the string until it becomes tightly twisted.

Then, slip all four fingers in the other end as well, and gently move your hands back and forth facing each other in a smooth, rhythmic motion. The whirrer should begin to spin very fast and to hum. If you color a simple geometric pattern on both sides of the disc, it will look very pretty as it whirls around.

Similar objects have been made in all parts of the world since the earliest times. They can be made from wood or bone, and holes can be drilled in them or the edges can be serrated to make different sounds. They have been called Bull roarers, Thunderspells, or Monsters.

When they are spinning around, they have the same action as a circular saw, so be careful how you use them!

Enjoy trying some of the activities and games suggested in this book. Ask other people what games with rope and string they know, and try to make up some new ones of your own. If you are interested in making things from string, look for books about Macrame, String Embroidery, and Curve Stitching.

Glossary

ceremony   A special occasion with traditional actions and speeches. Often concerned with religion.

hops   Plants used in brewing beer.

migrate   Wild birds migrate; they make a regular, instinctive journey and travel many miles from one part of the world to another to find a suitable climate for their survival at different times of the year.

Purgatory   In the beliefs of the Roman Catholic church, a place where the souls of the dead have to suffer for their sins before going to heaven.

taut   Stretched tightly.

territory   The land or space which a person, an animal, or a group regard as their own.

Vikings   Warlike Scandinavian traders and pirates who roamed the oceans around Europe from the eighth to tenth centuries.

Index of Countries

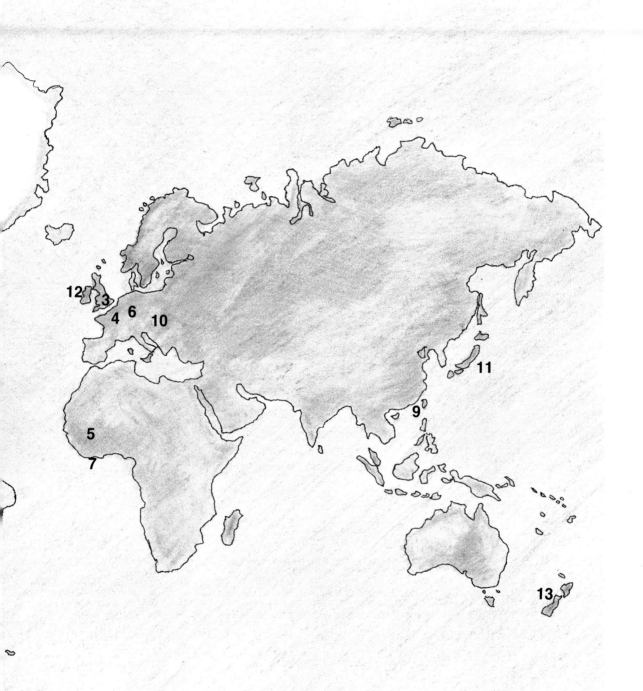

Index